Pop Culture presents the story of...

JEWEL

For more information, write to:

Power Publishing Limited
Kumar House
33 Newman Street
London W1P 3PO England
Telephone: 0171 255 3888
Fax: 0171 637 1906

The author and publisher have made every effort to contact all copyright holders. Any, who for whatever reason have not been contacted are invited to write to the publishers so that a full acknowledgement may be made in subsequent editions of this work.

Exclusive Distributors:

Omnibus Press
a Division of Music Sales Corporation
257 Park Avenue South
New York, New York 10010 USA

This edition published 1998 by Power Publishing Ltd.

ISBN 0.8256.1685.9

Picture credits: All Action, Gregg De Guire, Lisa O'Connor, Retna Pictures Limited, Rex Features Limited, Starfile, Tammie Arroyo

Cover Picture: All Action

Design by: Pop Culture

Printed in the United States of America by
Vicks Lithograph and Printing Corporation

Pop Culture presents the story of...

JEWEL

by Mark Bego

dedication

To Marie Morreale, amongst friends, you too are a shining jewel!

acknowledgements

The author would like to thank the following people:

Robert Bennett
Trippy Cunningham
Acrelda Farrell
A.J. Flick
Glenn Hughes
Marcy MacDonald
Sindi Markoff
Michael Shain
Zi Siddique
Ann Watt

contents

chapter one

whowill
saveyoursoul

She's part troubadour, part willowy waif, part sexy song stylist, and part rock star. Her music is introspective and poignantly moving. Her expressive writing tells tales of how love can be bracingly reassuring one minute, and devastatingly heartbreaking the next. She composes and performs her very personal and deeply moving songs from a very spiritual place, that echoes her own roller-coaster life of hard work, disappointments, and finally artistic redemption. She has brought folk music back into focus in the 1990s in a big way, and her name is Jewel.

Neither conventional nor predictable, her songs and her remarkable life are one of the most riveting musical success stories of the decade. Jewel Kilcher was born and raised in Alaska and, at the age of 24, has lived a lifetime of experiences. The daughter of folk singers in the town of Homer, Jewel and her brothers were raised in a home without running water or flush toilets. She honed her craft by yodeling on-stage with her parents as a little girl, and she quickly picked up her own honest and pure singing style. She weathered her parents' divorce, joined a rap group, and was even adopted by a local Indian tribe. As a teenager she moved to Hawaii for a very brief time, and then she won a musical scholarship to study in Michigan. By the early 1990s, she found herself broke and living in her car in San Diego, California. As she began to turn her touching poetry into songs to perform, she used a local coffee house as a showcase opportunity for herself. Like Blanche DuBois in *A Streetcar Named Desire*, she relied "on the kindness of strangers" for the use of a shower and a facility to wash out her clothes. She often had to use the sink of a public

chapter one

washroom at department stores to wash her hair. Yet, through it all, her soul, her spirit, and her integrity remained intact. She never lost sight of her goals, and after years of singing in front of enthusiastic audiences, finally her conviction's paid off.

Her debut album, 'Pieces Of You,' has sold over 8 million copies in America alone, and has interpreted into a huge multi-media career. Ever since it was released in February of 1995, she has gone on from one success to another. In November of that same year she starred as Dorothy in an all-rock-star version of *The Wizard Of Oz*. In 1997 she was nominated for two Grammy Awards and that summer was one of the stars of the all-girl Lilith Fair Festival tour of America. Now, in 1998, she is about to make her film debut in a major motion picture.

Five years ago, she was waiting tables in a restaurant, scraping leftover food from other people's plates, and rinsing out her clothes in the ladies' room at department stores. Now, she is one of the most successful new singers of the decade, with one of the most promising careers in the entertainment business. However, her friends will all attest to the fact that Jewel is still the same sweet girl she always was, even when she was down to her last dime.

Looking back on her own life, Jewel proudly claims, "Everything I've ever learned - good and bad - has given immeasurably to what I'm doing now.

I believe I've been guided and helped, and it's very humbling. I think if you demand, 'This is how I want my life to become,' it will. Miracles do happen." She ought to know, she is living proof of that theorem.

Nowadays, fans see her as the beautiful blonde on magazine covers, and in feature articles. However, things were not always so chic and lovely. She is the first to admit that her life has been far from glamorous. On a recent America On Line celebrity chat, she summed up the details of her past life and jobs as being, "Bucking hay bales, ditch digging, cow milking, waitressing, secretary... which I sucked at!" While audiences find her to be alluring and sexy in concert, Jewel herself is the first to downplay her attractiveness. "I don't really think about my sexuality on stage," she says. "I just sing. Singing is by nature very personal; it's an intensely intimate thing to watch somebody do. It is very sensual. It's very emotive. It's sad that the only time we're emotional with each other is usually when we're physically intimate. I think that people tend to confuse emotionalism with sexualism. Just because we're kind of repressed."

Although it would be easy for a folk singer of her "instant stardom" stature to become self-absorbed in her own life and her own feelings, Jewel is able to look at the lives of others, and relate their experiences as well. According to her, "One of my favorite things to do is sit and watch people. I make up their lives to be tragic or boring or brilliant." Her songs about others, like 'Adrian' and 'Painters' tell the stories of part-fictional, part-real characters, with a unifying world-wise spin that comes from her own unique perspective. She seems to have the ability to take a thought or a scenario, and turn it into a poetic display of emotion with universal feelings, accessible to a wide audience.

Explaining her own appeal, Jewel is the first to admit that her simplicity is one of her greatest selling points. "I'm not produced. I'm not slick. I don't have a big image thing," she proudly proclaims. "I'm a writer. It's probably from reading so much at a young age that my brain is shaped in a certain pattern."

chapter one

who will save your soul

chapter two

whowill**save**your**soul**

She also credits the values that both of her parents have instilled in her. With regard to her mother, Jewel explains, "She's always urged me to know myself and to be brave and to listen to myself. She'd urge me to spend five days alone in a cabin without anyone coming by, without any TV. I thought I'd go insane. And she'd have me do juice fasts and things like that."

The last three years have been like the fulfilment of a dream to Jewel. She didn't enter into an entertainment career simply for the money, she was attracted to it for the creativity and honesty of it. This whole acceptance of her art has only been sweetened by her new-found financial independence. Her poetry has been written with colorful brushstrokes, as though she was painting a picture on an audible canvas. Speaking of her success, she claims, "It made me so happy. And to tell you the truth, that's what has always led me through life... I always knew that there would be a chord that would match up to the colors. A lot of my life was spent without it being matched, but I feel like now I've struck the chord."

According to Jewel, her favorite word is "ubiquitous." Taken literally, it means to be universally everywhere at once. It is the perfect term to use to describe this colorful and fascinating singer, because she too is everywhere at once. As she herself laughs, "'Ubiquitous.' It sounds just great, and it rhymes with ridiculous."

And, ridiculously ubiquitously successful is exactly what she has become. Yet, with over 8 million copies of her debut album sold, Jewel still harbors some self-doubts about her own brilliance. "My thoughts aren't that original," she says in an almost apologetic tone. "My emotions aren't that original. Everybody has thought what I've thought. It's not like I'm harboring some hidden human emotion that no one else has had and I better keep it to myself." What she is doing, however, is reaching inside herself, and illuminating the dark corners of her own emotions, universalizing them, and shedding an incandescent light on them.

Yes, everyone has felt sadness. Yes, everyone has had self-doubts. Yes, everyone has fears. And, occasionally, everyone has gone off into a depression, stared up at the sky and has wondered, "What the hell does my life all mean in the grand scheme of things?" However, it is Jewel's artistic strength to have the ability to take these thoughts and feelings, internalize them, and then crystallize them into highly personal story-songs that can somehow touch all of our hearts, minds and souls.

chapter two

little
sisterinalaska

She's been called "the wonder from the Tundra," in the press, and in a way, that is what Jewel has been acknowledged as being. Speaking of her hometown, she explains, "Homer, Alaska, is where I'm from. It's beautiful, with a lot of mountains and water and meadows. It's a small town of only five hundred people, but it's quite cosmopolitan and artistic."

Homer is located southwest of Anchorage, on the Kenai Peninsula, west of the Reni Mountains, and near the Kachemak Bay State Park. Like all of the state of Alaska, Homer is filled with interesting characters, and a breathtaking landscape. "Just a funny little town,"says Jewel. "There's this guy, Stinky, that you can visit. He lives in a junkyard. There's a refrigerator, which is on its back, and you yell, 'Stinky!' The refrigerator opens, and up walks Stinky out of the earth!"

Since the winters are so long, and the summers are so short, when she is asked what her favorite holiday is, she replies, "Easter. In Alaska, it means that spring is coming, which everyone's very happy about."

Speaking of her heritage, Jewel says, "My grandfather moved to Alaska before it was a state - he was one of the first settlers." In fact, grandpa Yule Kilcher, who emigrated to the 49th State from Switzerland, still occasionally rides his horse and buggy into town when his automobile fails to run. He homesteaded 800 acres of land, and that's where he raised his family.

Jewel's father, Atz Kilcher, is a Vietnam War veteran and social worker. Her mother, Nedra, is a glass artist. Together, Atz and Nedra raised Jewel and her two brothers, and moonlighted as folk singers at local bars and restaurant lounges, often dragging along their children for the ride.

little sister in alaska

Of the three siblings, it was Jewel who soon found that she was the most musically inclined child in the family. By the time she was 6 years old, she was officially part of her parents' act.

The family lived together in a log cabin, without either electricity or plumbing. The closest thing they had to running water, was when they hooked up a garden hose to a nearby running stream. Looking back on her life in Homer, Jewel explains, "It was not a hippie thing. It was like pioneers, when people moved West. We had a hose, and you hooked it up to the stream. But if there were worms - because the stream flooded, there were worms in your faucet."

Because of this, baths for the Kilcher family became a weekly ritual. They would all load themselves into the car and drive 20 miles to a community sauna and pool, for some liquid immersion. She recalls, "It was an education, too, to see red pubic hair for the first time. It was like, 'Whoa! I didn't know it could be like that.'"

Although it sounds like a potentially romantic lifestyle, Jewel is the first to explain, "Look, it was a lot of work. We'd be canning salmon after school while other kids would be watching *He-Man* (on television). But, I was also very proud of it, and it shaped me into a certain kind of person. You'd get up at 5 in the morning, and there would be frost on your eyelashes. I shared a room with my brothers. I'd cook breakfast, milk the cow, walk three miles to the road, hitch-hike to school. It was a romantic and poetic existence"

Without either electricity or television, Jewel had to rely on her own imagination for entertainment. "Look at it like a science project," she says. "I was spared a lot of media. I was spared a lot of fear talk. I'm aware now how affected I am when I hear on the news how violent we (the human race) are, how we can't trust our religious or political leaders. That affects your ability to interact as a person. I was spared that and instead given a natural curiosity about life." Recalling the earliest memory of her childhood, she recounts, "Well, I was in a basement - I don't know how I got down there - and there were all these colors in my head, shimmering and dancing, as color might. My mom goes, 'Jewel? Are you down there?' I remember consciously taking my name. And what was 'Jewel', were these colors and brightness in my head." Somehow, she always knew that she was meant to become a glittering gem amongst mere pebbles.

littlesisterinalaska

Although she loved the social interaction of attending school, she found that she had a bit of a learning disability. Expressing her childhood disappointment, she says, "Having dyslexia made me feel like I would never be interested in life again. I used to love reading when I was little, and then it became difficult and I didn't understand why. I thought, 'What a bummer, my passion all drained out of me.' So when I found out I had dyslexia it was like, oh, that's what it was."

Her only exposure to outside music came from the radio. She knew very little about rock & roll, but somehow jazz permeated the snowdrifts of the Alaska winters. Speaking of her earliest musical influences, Jewel says, "What really got me into perfecting my voice and stuff was Ella Fitzgerald - just listening to her ability, her skill. Ella Fitzgerald's voice I enjoyed more than Billie (Holiday)'s, because it was more versatile and more playful. It just made me feel better to listen to her."

Even from a very early age, Jewel had no concept of the phenomenon of "stage fright." As she explains it, "I've been performing live since I was 6 years old. I was very driven. We toured Eskimo villages and I yodeled - it was just a novelty thing. People have always liked yodeling."

Although she is talented at the art of yodeling, sometimes it did get her into trouble. "My father is Swiss, so I guess it's in my blood," she says. "When I was in third grade, I got kicked out of class for yodeling."

According to Atz Kilcher, "She's just really had a knack for it. She was always a quick learner, very hard-working and tenacious. Anything I'd tell her to do with her voice, she could do. One time when she was about 6, she was yodeling with us at a hotel show, and this lady came up and said she was a professor of music. She told us it was supposed to be impossible for a child like that to be able to yodel - as a child's vocal chords hadn't developed properly yet."

The first rock album that she recalls hearing was from the group Pink Floyd, with their classic LP, 'The Wall.' "I was 6," she says, I thought it was *Pink Panther*. Which is pretty funny to think that the Pink Panther was going around singing, 'All in all, it's just another brick in the wall.'"

Along
the   way,
Atz   and   Nedra
Kilcher   were   able   to
record   two   albums   of   their
own folk music. Now that Jewel is
a huge success in the recording business,
collectors will be scouring record bins for 'Early
Morning Gold' (1977) and 'Raised On Alaska Land'
(1978) by the duo.

chapter two   little sister in alaska

Jewel remembers her early childhood as being very relaxed and
easygoing. Both of her parents gave her and her brothers a free rein in
their after-school activities. "My dad was always like, 'Do whatever you want,'
but my mom would say, 'Be home by 9:00,'" she says.

It wasn't long before her love of music and yodeling gave way to her vocalizing. She was
especially encouraged by her father to learn to sing more proficiently. "We'd practice - at my own
will - for five hours a day," Jewel explains. "At 7 or 8 years old, I was doing these really sophisticated
bluegrass harmonies. My dad was a real entertainers' entertainer: He would chide me for not moving around
on stage. He never wrote a set list - he said you had to read the crowd's mood." She adopted this same theory for
playing to a crowd. Today she proudly proclaims, "I never write a set list."

Her life however, made a swift change when her parents separated, and her mother moved away. As she explains it, "Until I
was 8, my upbringing was very normal."

Jewel was just old enough to be very disturbed by the family splitting up. "It was very unreal. I lost all equilibrium," she
painfully recalls. "Leaving your mom on a street corner while you drive away in the a back of a car is just... brutal. And
my dad at that time was out-to-lunch, bless his heart."

Her mother had always taught her about art and poetry and music, and those influences have stayed
with her even when they were apart during this period of time. Says Jewel, "Through those
lessons, I was given a tool. After my parents got divorced, I started writing poetry a lot
because I didn't always know how to express myself. That, to me, is the real beauty
of writing; it makes you more intimate with yourself."

Since the divorce, Atz continued to perform as a solo act. He would then have
his daughter join him on stage. He never had to ask Jewel twice if she
wanted to come up and sing and yodel and play with him in front
of the audience. "I always had a choice," she claims, "I really
did. People always think, 'Oh, an 8-year-old in a bar,'
but it wasn't like that. I didn't feel unsafe. It was
more family-restaurant bars. My brothers
didn't do it. I was the one that liked
to practice five hours a day. It
definitely   wasn't   a
boredom thing. I
loved it."

littlesisterinalaska

She really threw herself into learning to play the guitar, and singing. Speaking of her dyslexia, Jewel says, "Because of my history, it's hard for me to learn things, so I practised twenty times as hard."

Very often she learned life lessons by watching others make fatal mistakes with their own lives. "I saw women who would compromise themselves for compliments, for flattery; or men who would run away from themselves by drinking until they ultimately killed themselves," says Jewel.

Then there was the bizarre incident with the local pervert with a camera. Apparently, a man in Homer approached Atz and told him that he wanted to photograph his daughter. "My dad was flattered. He's flattered that I am cute, which is sweet, but..." Jewel recounts. "So I went there to the man's trailer, and he puts me in a dress and combs my hair out. I was so uncomfortable, and I told my dad I didn't like the man. Later it turns out that the man was in the paper as a child pornographer and molester. My dad came to me crying, and said, "I will never doubt your instincts again.""

Throughout this era, it was music that really bound Jewel to her father. "We really had singing in common, so I sang my little brains out," she says. "Plus, I loved singing. He'd scream and curse, and I'd be crying, and I'd still sit there and practice."

With all that wonderful wilderness surrounding the family cabin, Jewel had lots of room to pursue one of her favorite, life-long passions, horseback riding. When asked to name her favorite childhood pet, she fondly replies, "My horse, Clearwater. He was my escape as a kid when things got hard. When I got him, he was really sick, and everybody said he wouldn't live. But I just pampered him and nurtured him. He's about 12 now, and my dad takes care of him back in Homer."

As a young girl, she also immersed herself in reading. According to her, her favorite author is: "Kurt Vonnegut Jr. He is the master of the short story. I love reading him because he is really straight to the point and very inventive. I especially like his *Welcome To The Monkey House.*"

Although she was isolated in Alaska, Jewel claims that some pop icons permeated the Tundra. According to her, "I knew who Cyndi Lauper was. I knew what blue eyeliner was!"

With her mother gone, Jewel began to feel a bit out of place in the rugged wilderness, especially after she reached puberty. Her body was changing, but her father and brothers were unaware that "little sister" was growing up. "I lived with all guys," she claims. "I didn't tell anybody. You just kind of shave your legs in the dark by yourself, embarrassed. And I didn't have any privacy, either. We had outhouses, you know? It wasn't a great place to become a woman. No matter how hard my life was with my family, it just gave me such tremendous spirituality and comfort. You knew there was a God. You knew there was some good force in the world, and you were lucky to be a part of it, safely."

When she was 14 years old, Jewel joined a local amateur rap group that called itself 'La Creme'. As she explains, "My boyfriend at the time, Damien, was in the group. They called me Swiss Miss. When my father met Damien, the first black boyfriend I ever had, he was in tears." According to her, what Atz said to her was, "I'm so proud that I raised such an open-minded daughter."

Now a teenager, Jewel found that she was having feelings and frustrations that she had trouble expressing. "It got to the point where if I had a problem with my father, I could never speak it. I would write four pages and give it to him."

Unsatisfied with her home life, she became close with several of the local Native American Indians. She soon found herself adopted by the tribe. As she explains it, "[They] took me out to a meadow and said, 'Your life in the future will call for you to speak honestly to people. You don't know how to speak from your heart, and you need to learn how.' I remember going on top of a mountain and trying to say anything honest - just to the wind. I was crying because I couldn't say anything sincere."

According to her, she gleaned a lot of her spirituality from the experience. "The American Indian thing had a big influence on me," she claims. "You adopt the Indian way. Everybody is your uncle or aunt."

Two of her new "uncles" were very wise and influential members of the Ottawa tribe. Jewel recalls, "One said I was going to bring heart to the people."

Very often, the simple truths of spiritual people, like the Ottawa Indians, make more sense, and hold more reality than any scientifically measured facts. Somehow her Native American "uncle" must have seen into the future and read a *Billboard* magazine album chart from the 1990s, because this Jewel in the rough, was destined to do exactly that.

anangel
standingby

◆◆◆◆◆◆◆◆◆◆◆◆◆◆◆◆◆◆◆◆◆◆◆◆◆◆◆◆◆◆◆◆◆◆◆◆◆

Finally, at the age of 15, Jewel had enough of living in a log cabin in Homer, Alaska. There was a whole world outside of her little hometown, and she wanted to see some of it - immediately. According to her, "I was tired of the cold, and my dad!"

So, she packed up her bags and headed for the tropical splendor of the 50th State, Hawaii. However, the land of pineapples and grass skirts was less than friendly to this singer from the land of the permafrost. "I would almost get beaten up every day by the Hawaiian kids because I was white," she recalls of her tropical misadventure. "It was my first time dealing with prejudice. I was stuck there until I could earn enough money to go home."

She worked at odd jobs until she scraped together the airfare, and returned to Alaska. However, instead of going to Homer, she went to live in Anchorage with her mother, Nedra. Although it was nice to be back with her mother, and to be in the "big city" of Anchorage, it wasn't the bed of roses she had envisaged.

Her mother was still pursuing her career as a glass artist in Alaska's largest city. She had gone into business with a partner, and apparently there were shady dealings relating to the partner. Nedra was investigated by the FBI, causing a local scandal. Says Jewel, "Investigators would come to my school, and there would be things on her in the paper. We ended up having to hock our stuff and move 200 miles away."

Together, Nedra and her daughter moved to the town of Seward, Alaska. As Jewel recounts the experience, "I was facing my 16th year of life, and I was really desperate. I kept thinking, 'What am I going to do with myself? I had a sense that something needed to happen or else I would suffocate."

A friend of hers was enrolled in the prestigious Interlochen Fine Arts Academy in the northern part of the lower peninsula of Michigan. Talking to the friend, a light went off in Jewel's head, and she decided that she wanted to attend the school as well, and really hone her craft. She lined up a partial scholarship for herself, but she also needed to come up with cash as well to clinch the deal. She and Nedra put their heads together, and came up with a scheme to finance Jewel's musical education. They arranged for a concert in Homer, attended by all of their local friends and neighbors, and when it was over, they passed around the hat. It was a gamble, but it paid off. She packed her bags and left Alaska for Michigan.

Interlochen was just the kind of polish that she needed to make the advancement from singing as a hobby, to singing and playing the guitar masterfully and expressively. As she explains of the experience, "I saw a bigger world. I immersed myself in everything - drama, dance, sculpture, music."

In the meantime, Nedra had relocated south to San Diego, California. When Jewel's studies were over, she boarded a train, and headed down there as well. However, she was soon disappointed to find out that although California was an area of great opportunity, just arriving there unannounced didn't make it "the land of milk and honey."

By the time Jewel reached San Diego, she found Nedra in the same financial boat - broke. What followed was a string of odd jobs, including waitressing. When faced with making a big decision - an apartment or a vehicle - Jewel borrowed money from a boyfriend, and opted for a 1979 Volkswagen van. Not only did she drive the van, but she lived in it. And what about Nedra? Did she leave her mother behind? No. She lived in the van parked next to Jewel's!

an
angel
standing
by

As Jewel explains it, "We could have gotten an apartment. It was a decision not to do that, it was freedom. If I could afford an apartment, I couldn't afford a car. If I could afford to pay rent, I couldn't afford food. I'm not exaggerating. So you can imagine that having that burden gone was tremendous. I found a favorite spot that was near a little flowering tree. I pulled my van up close so the tree hit the window and nobody could see in. And you light candles and you read at night."

And what about things like flush toilets and running water? According to Jewel, "I grew up without all that. It wasn't a difficult thing for me or my mom. Running water? Who cares?"

Without a bathroom of their own, Jewel and her mother would have to go to department stores and shopping malls, and use the public bathrooms to wash their hair and use the facilities.

She absolutely hated being a waitress. "When you're so poor that you can't find food, and you're scraping food off

people's plates in restaurants to take home, it's degrading. And I would let bosses flirt with me, because they would take me out to dinner. I'd say, 'I'm not interested in you.' But, you still played the game."

After a while, she felt her spirit start to become burdened by the desolation of it all. Thankfully, San Diego is at least a beautiful city to be broke and destitute in. She even took up surfing in the Pacific Ocean. According to her, "I'm a long-boarder; I'm not great but I can do a bottom turn."

"Despite my surroundings," says Jewel, "this was a difficult time for me. I felt a lot of social pressure to figure out what I was gonna do with the rest of my life. I had no desire to go to college, but I also felt no peace in traveling or just bumming around. I got a number of dead-end jobs - got fired a couple of times. I was frightened and a little depressed. The idea of spending my life in a 9-to-5 job made me feel trapped and hopeless."

Then,
there was
always the possibility
of going back to school.
"My mom kept challenging me. I'd
say, 'I have to go to school,' and my mom
kept saying, 'What do you want? What does your
spirit say?' Finally I said, 'I know what I want. I want to
sing until people never feel alone.' And when I said that, she
said, 'OK.'"
Now she had to get focused. One of the guys she met during this era was Steve
Poltz, who was a member of a local band called The Rugburns. He was startled to find
how musically unaware Jewel was. She had never listened to Joni Mitchell, and could not even
recognize a Beatles tune on the radio. According to Poltz, "When I met her in San Diego, she was, like,
this social misfit. Once I was with her, and 'I Want To Hold Your Hand,' I think, came on the radio, and she
said, 'Now, what's this band called? Is this The [Rolling] Stones?' And she was deadly serious. I said, 'This is The
Beatles.' She was like, 'Oh! I like it!'"
In time, Steve became her musical mentor. As she tells it, "My friend Steve from The Rugburns has been instrumental. I'd never heard
the Replacements. I'd never heard the Beatles' 'White Album.' He sat me down and had what he called Jewel 101 classes."
She soon found that Poltz was more of a creatively nurturing friend than a boyfriend. "It's not meant to be that
way. It's not always about sex," she explains. "We write incredible songs together. It makes me get
goosebumps."
When she lost her waitressing job, Jewel and Nedra were really down on their luck. They
didn't even have enough money to pay for medicine if one of them became ill.
According to Jewel, "Once I let a kidney infection go too long, and we went
to all these doctors' offices and they'd refuse me. Antibiotics are $60
to $100. I'm in the car, throwing up all over myself, and my
mom would get refused by one clinic after another.
And seeing my mom walk out of the clinics
was damaging to my spirit. It just
made you angry. Nobody
gave a sh**. Nobody
had to."

Although
the Bohemian
lifestyle that they were
living sounds uncomplicated
and romantic, being broke and
living in your van isn't all that it's cracked
up to be. "I was scared. I was 18, and I thought
I would have to give up everything I believed in and
everything I wanted to do. I just hated life. I cried every day.
It was so frustrating."

She was at a turning point in her life, and she knew it. "I told myself, 'OK,
I'm going to do something I love or I'm going to die,'" she claims. At the time she
and her mother were surviving on carrot sticks and peanut butter. A big meal out
consisted of a grazing session at the Happy Hour buffet table of a local bar. A luxury bathing
experience consisted of splashing water on herself in the lavatory of the local K-Mart. The ladies' room
of the Denny's restaurant at the intersection of Gabriel and Mission was another favorite bathing spa.

Understandably, Jewel felt like her life was a mess, circa 1994. Although she was enjoying surfing
and writing her poetry, she knew that she was going nowhere - fast. Enter: The Innerchange
Coffeehouse. This is where her entire life was destined to change. At the age of 19 she
began performing there regularly, and within weeks of singing her introspective
story-songs there, she had gained quite a following. "They were an
amazing audience," she recalls, "from 8 to 80 years old. That's what
I want my fan base to be."

She was a huge hit the first time she played at the coffee
house. Such a big hit in fact, that several of the
other musicians invited her to sing and play
on stage during their sets, as a
"guest" artist. The next thing
she knew, she was
offered her own
weekly gig.

She and Nedra were still living in their vans, but somehow she always ended up with exactly what she needed, at precisely the right time. "I learned to pray, and I learned to manifest things," says Jewel. "People would help out. If I said, 'Angels,' or whoever, I really need a place to take a shower,' I'd meet a guy in a coffee shop who was really nice. He'd give me the key to his apartment and would let me take showers before shows."

It wasn't long before she began to attract a loyal following of people who loved her music. Word of mouth reviews helped to spread the word. Slowly, her attitude about her life began to change, and she concentrated on her singing career. "It's so easy to feel alone and to feel like you're the only one going through whatever you're going through," she ponders. "You feel very isolated in it - especially when you're young, when you're around 18. When I was that age, I was amazed and so thankful for what little pieces of encouragement I got. It was profoundly affecting. I know that my music does that."

Critics and audience members alike, flocked to see Jewel. One of her first glowing reviews came from the local San Diego magazine, 'Slamm.' The publication proclaimed, "Her voice is many things, all of them beautiful. When she opens up, the sound is crystalline and pure."

One night, a woman by the name of Inga Vainschtein came into the Innerchange Coffeehouse, and was absolutely mesmerized by the willowy blonde girl she witnessed singing there.

According to Vainschtein, "The first time I saw her perform, she reminded me of Barbra Streisand meets Meryl Streep." A former film executive, it was Inga who first brought Jewel to the attention of Atlantic Records.

Jewel has always claimed that she believed in miracles. Well, somehow the angels looked down on her, and a miracle had just occurred. Voila...! Within five months of her Innerchange debut, Jewel was signed to her own recording deal!

a shimmering jewel

◆◆◆◆◆◆◆◆◆◆◆◆◆◆◆◆◆◆◆◆◆◆◆◆◆◆◆◆◆◆◆◆◆◆◆◆◆

After being broke for so long, what did Jewel do with her first paycheck? According to her, "I was real tight about spending money. Always have been. I don't think I really bought anything. I moved into an apartment. I bought a used car." Well, she was on her way now. Atlantic Records immediately put her debut album in motion, and she began recording tracks.

The producer that they placed at the helm of this project was Ben Keith, who is best known for his work with Neil Young, and his phenomenally successful albums 'Harvest' and 'Harvest Moon.' Some of the tracks were recorded at the Innerchange Coffeehouse in San Diego, and the studio tracks were recorded in Neil's own studio, Redwood Digital at Broken Arrow Ranch in Woodside, California.

Not only did Neil Young lend his studio and his producer to Jewel, but he also threw in his back-up band, The Stray Gators (Spooner Oldman, Tim Drummond, and Oscar Butterworth) for several of the cuts. It seems that a little bit of Neil's good karma must have rubbed off on the project, as it was destined to become the biggest selling folk album of the 1990's!

Looking back on her 'Pieces Of You' album, Jewel claims, "It's really a time capsule. When I recorded it, I thought, 'No one's gonna hear it. I'm just going to be honest and put it down on tape.' I didn't really clean up all the edges."

Although, Jewel in retrospect claims it "has tons of mistakes in it," the fact that it isn't slick or over produced makes it very real and accessible.

'Pieces Of You' was released in February 1995, and it began its slow ascent up the record charts in *Billboard* magazine.

ashimmeringjewel

Ron Shapiro, a Vice President at Atlantic Records, recalls, "She was an unknown artist, and everybody at that time was saying that this was some little folk record from a little girl in Alaska. She was the hardest artist to break and took the longest to break in this company's history. The first year they spat on us. And in the most vitriolic way. It was basically, 'She's a woman, she's a folk artist - are you kidding?' And critics were saying the record had no merit."

Desperate to draw a parallel between Jewel and anyone who came before her, critics most commonly felt that she was the 1990s version of Joni Mitchell. The funny thing was that Jewel Kilcher had never even listened to 'Ladies Of The Canyon' nor 'Court And Spark.' "I'd never heard of Joni Mitchell before I did my album," she proclaims. "I'd heard a lot of Bob Dylan, Ella Fitzgerald. I wasn't raised in a vacuum - I did hear things on the radio, but I didn't have a lot of Bob Dylan, Ella Fitzgerald. I did hear things on the radio, but I didn't have a tape player. I've never been a real music fan. I'm odd that way. But the people I love, I totally studied. I studied Jennifer Warnes until I could do her voice perfectly."

She had spent all those years without running water or flush toilets - no sweat. But no Joni Mitchell? Unthinkable!

Although it was an uphill climb, she actually did begin to receive airplay. Almost universally, it was the song 'Who Will Save Your Soul' that started to make noise on the airwaves. Ron Shapiro explains, "At that point there were not that many women on alternative radio, and along comes a folk-pop record tinged with country - in other words, the very thing that these stations run farthest from."

Touring was the key to breaking Jewel through to her own audience. She began performing as many as three shows a day for different audiences, simply trying to gain attention. "I'd do a high school show in the morning, then I'd open for a gothic band, then a midnight show, drive three hours, sleep three hours - I was raised with hard work," she says.

Somehow, it all worked for her. She was astonished to be able to proclaim, "I manage to hold 20,000 people's attention between Everclear and the Ramones."

Looking back on the release of the album, Jewel is able to laugh, "When my record came out, it was like a little fizzle. The moment I can really remember is when I sold 8,000 records in one week. I remember crying on my kitchen floor, just thanking God that I might not ever have to waitress or live in my car again." The people at Atlantic Records were amazed at how hard Jewel was willing to work to promote the LP. She was tireless in her determination to make something of this opportunity. According to her, "I'm able to focus mercilessly for a long time because I was trained to do that at a young age. However, it's not like I worked this hard waitressing. I can work this hard because I had one shot at this. I really thought I would live in a car or probably have an apartment, but I thought I would live on that level my entire existence. I was given a shot and it all fell on my shoulders. I'm glad it did, because I knew I could do something about it."

Her own personal favorite track on the album is the song 'Amen.' She explains, "'Amen,' I think that lyrically, as a poem, it's very strong, and I like what it stands for. I wrote it for the death of Kurt Cobain - not so much for him but for his suicide following. He was definitely the hero for the heroless."

Although radio stations favored the more optimistic tunes, like 'Who Will Save Your Soul' and 'You Were Meant For Me,' it seemed like the album had something for everyone. The defiance of 'Daddy,' the heartbreak of 'Adrian,' and the bittersweet song of the death of a loved one, 'Painters,' all struck a universally emotional chord.

When one journalist asked Jewel what her songs were about, she simply replied, "Trying to figure out 'Where do I fit in in the world?'"

'I'm Sensitive' is another one she is very proud of having recorded. According to her, "I wrote that song because I was really hurt by something that happened with a musician I used to work with. And I just wanted to say, 'I do bleed, we all do. Don't be cruel to people - it isn't a talent.' But I have a real cheese alert, and I was never gonna put it on the album because there's no way in hell I'm gonna get away with saying that in public. But in my coffee-shop shows, people responded to it so strongly that despite myself I put it on. I was like, 'Get off it, Jewel. Take a few hits. If it helps people, do it ya'know?'"

chapter four a**shimmering**jewel

Almost immediately Jewel found herself on the same bill with very intense rock bands, but like she said, she managed to hold everyone's attention in between the head-bangers. Was life on the road wild for her? Did she party her brains out? Not exactly. "I don't drink," she explains, "I have problems with my kidneys, and it's never interested me, anyway. I mean, after a show, I usually go back to the hotel and get into my pajamas."

In May 1995 she made one of her first national television appearances on *The Late Show With Conan O'Brien*. The great thing about national television is the fact that you never really know who is watching you. One of the people who was sitting in front of his television that night, was none other than Sean Penn. He immediately tracked Jewel down, and invited her to join him at the Venice Film Festival.

At the time, Sean had broken up with his live-in girlfriend, Robin Wright. For several months, Sean and Jewel dated and were a romantic couple. He even directed the original video for her song, 'You Were Meant For Me.' According to her, "He saw me perform on 'Conan O'Brien' and called me up to ask me to do a song for his movie *The Crossing Guard*." Speaking of Penn, she illuminates, "He's very kind, professional and efficient, and the shots (in the video) were beautiful."

Ultimately, after several months together as an "item," they broke up. Sean went back to Robin - the mother of his two children - and they got married. Jewel ended up going back to Steve Poltz. Career-wise, things were very hectic for her. Throughout that year, Jewel literally took every gig that she could. Anything to play her music in front of an audience. One of the most bizarre projects she got involved in was a rock & roll/Broadway version of *The Wizard Of Oz*, which aired on cable TV station TNT in November 1995. The Tin Man was played by Roger Daltry, the Cowardly Lion was portrayed by Nathan Lane, and Jewel was Dorothy.

What a strange parallel to Jewel's own life this production was. She had been taken from a Kansas-like drab existence in her Volkswagen van, and suddenly she found herself on stage singing and dancing with one of the members of the group The Who. Yes, Jewel, there is no place like rock & roll!

The album just kept selling and selling. First it went Gold in America (500,000 copies sold), then Platinum (1,000,000 copies sold). The next thing she knew she was the opening act for such rock legends as Bob Dylan, and Neil Young. According to her, "I was so nervous about playing Madison Square Garden with (Neil Young). He said, 'Jewel, it's just another hash house on the road to success. Show it no respect."

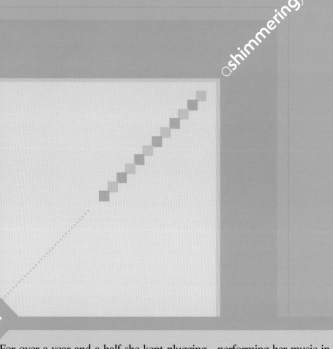

For over a year and a half she kept plugging - performing her music in front of more and more audiences. She was heard singing the song 'Sunshine Superman' on the soundtrack album for the movie, *I Shot Andy Warhol*. In 1997 she was on the *Batman & Robin* soundtrack singing "Foolish Games." She starred on MTV's hit series *Unplugged*. She was the musical guest on *Saturday Night Live*. She performed on David Letterman's show, and then she was on the all-guest-star album of music from the hit late night TV series. In 1997 she was invited to perform at one of the Washington D.C. parties for President Bill Clinton's second inaugural celebration. All of a sudden she is all over the place. She had become the personification of her favorite word, "ubiquitous."

One of her most controversial appearances came in February of 1997, when she was seen on the annual Grammy Awards telecast. Up for two separate trophies, she unfortunately didn't win. However, her appearance caused quite a stir. In an uncharacteristic glamour move, Jewel borrowed a $14,000 dress from famed designer Gianfranco Ferre. She looked absolutely stunning in the dress when she put it on in her hotel room. It was low-cut, and sparkled with sequins and beads, and appeared to be made of a filmy, dreamy, gauze-like material. What she didn't realize was the fact that she was going to be backlit on stage, and much to everyone's surprise, the dress became translucent. As it wasn't the kind of dress one wears undergarments with, and... well, you get the picture.

ashimmeringjewel

"I didn't know it was see-through!" she later exclaimed. She didn't have a clue that it would turn diaphanous in the spotlights. By the time she figured it out, it was too late. "That whole thing with the Grammys was hilarious. The dress... I wasn't backlit in the hotel room. You're in a dress, you feel like an angel. I didn't have the entire spotlight up my ass. I still haven't looked at the video tape."

Fortunately, she has a good sense of humor. "I felt angelic in it," she further explains. "Every girl has a fantasy to play dress-up. I want to be allowed to experiment in front of the world. People were like, 'You can't be sensitive and sexy.' But I refuse to be burdened by my womanhood. Anyway, you end up trying these things on in hotel rooms, which aren't backlit."

Although she did not win either of the Grammy Awards she was nominated for, it was still an exciting evening. Her date for the night was her first favorite folk singer, her dad, Atz Kilcher. "He went to the Grammys with me," she proudly announces. "He toured with me and taped VH1's *Hard Rock Live* with me. The last time I was on stage with him, I was looking up at him because I was so much littler. And then to have him on my stage with my crowd... it was staggering."

The next big piece of exposure that Jewel received in 1997, was as part of the highly successful all-girl Lilith Fair Festival concert tour. Alongside such women as Sarah McLaughlin, Jewel won hearts and sold albums like hotcakes.

When she was asked at the time, how the Lilith Fair Festival women have changed the perception of the male-dominated rock world, Jewel answered modestly, "There have been so many women before us - Janis Joplin, Patti Smith. The real women in rock were way before us. I kinda feel like we don't really count," she laughs. "As far as my success as compared to Janis Joplin, I think only time will tell. I still have to prove myself. As far as the rest (of the 1990s rock women), yeah, I'm sure that the success has helped. The Lilith Fair Festival has given promoters the idea that we can make money and all those business things."

Jewel is so entirely different from other female rockers, like Madonna, or Courtney Love, that using all three names in the same sentence seems odd. When asked what she personally thinks of the "Material Girl," she answers, "My favorite quote is Liz Phair's. She said, 'Madonna is a speedboat, and the rest of us are just The Go-Go's on water skis.' Madonna just paved the way in so many ways. She was never afraid to break down taboos. I think she's very intelligent, incredibly business-savvy. And she taught a lot of women of my generation to believe in what they've got. My only fear is that people might have interpreted what she's done, or what artists have done since her, (as being) 'Sex is our power.' Not that I think you have to be clad in blue jeans and a white T-shirt to be a sincere woman rocker. It's just that (we should be) making sure that we're relying on our talent and not our breasts."

Are women in rock & roll treated differently from the men? "Yeah, definitely. It's always existed. Men are allowed, in rock & roll, to get up and look great all unshaved. I think because sex is what interests America, when you think of women, you look for sex more for some reason. Probably because of 'Playboy' (magazine) and that whole mentality."

The Lilith Fair Festival tour was very significant for Jewel. In many people's eyes, she emerged the biggest star of it. When *Time* magazine interviewed her for a piece on the festival, it was Jewel whom they put on the cover of their July 21, 1997 issue, with the headline: "JEWEL AND THE GANG - Macho music out. Empathy is in. And the all-female Lilith festival is taking rock's hot new sound on the road."

The fact that Jewel is a beautiful woman has certainly helped her career. It is not sex that she is selling, but America is very "packaging" oriented. It is her music, and her insightful lyrics that have made her one of the most popular new artists of the decade. However, the fact that she is gorgeous has played a big hand in paving the way for the next turn on her own personal magical mystery tour - that of movie star.

a shimmering jewel

no**more** foolishgames

In September 1997, Jewel's 'You Were Meant For Me' video won MTV's award as the Best Female Video of the year. She was apparently on a winning streak. The following month, while she was on tour in Europe, her name was all over the covers of entertainment trade magazines like *Variety*, as she signed separate agreements to star in a new film, and to become the author of two forthcoming books.

The film deal came first. Budgeted at $35 million, film-maker Ang Lee announced that he had inked Jewel as the female star of the Civil War epic, *To Live On*, based on the novel, *Woe To Live On*, by David Woodrell. Jewel will portray the love interest of two soldiers fighting on the Kansas/Missouri border in the 1860s. Filming was set to start in March 1998.

With regard to making her big screen debut, Jewel claimed, "I'm really looking forward to having my ass kicked by a new challenge. For me, singing and songwriting utilize only one part of a very creative body."

In the October 30 issue of *The New York Post*, media writer Michael Shain reported, "Folksy rocker Jewel, whose debut album has been on the charts for nearly two years, will get a record $2 million to tell her life story. The advance... is believed to be as much - if not more - than any other pop musician has received for a memoir." With this phenomenal advance, Jewel surpassed the likes of autobiography advances paid to Aretha Franklin ($1.5 million), Grace Slick ($1 million), Aerosmith ($1 million), LeAnn Rimes ($1 million), and Gladys Knight ($500,000).

In actuality, Jewel was contracted for two separate books in the same deal. The first one is a book of her poetry, and the second one is a memoir and scrapbook of her life. Suddenly, she was more than just the singing Jewel, she was the multi-media millionairess precious Jewel!

chapter five

nomorefoolishgames

As of the beginning of 1998, the majority of Jewel's second album was already finished. However, Atlantic Records was hesitant to bring it out yet, as 'Pieces Of You' was still selling well, and they didn't want to knock it off the charts by having Jewel compete with herself. What a wonderful position to be in - to be so successful that your follow-up LP had to be held back till Autumn 1998.

This time around, she has turned to producer Peter Collins to assist her in the studio. Collins has previously worked with such diverse artists as Nanci Griffith, and Queensryche. I guess you could say that Jewel's music lies somewhere in the middle of these two extremes.

Giving a little preview of the much-anticipated disk, Jewel explains that it will feature "a lot more layering, a lot more texturing. My hands have caught up with my head now."

That's not all that's caught up in her life. Finally her bank account has caught up with her dreams. Just recently she took a vast sum of her money, and put a downpayment on her very own house in the San Diego area, known as Del Mar. She also bought herself a new car, a Volvo station wagon. She claims, "(It is) a great car 'cause you can still go out and sleep in the desert. Old habits die hard."

It doesn't sound like she will be back to sleeping in her car anytime soon. In fact, she even has the space for her own new quarter horse, whom she has named "Jazz." According to her, "Horseback riding is the most natural thing in my blood - that and singing."

She has even hypothesized about taking Jazz out on tour with her, in his own little trailer. "If Neil Young can go out with truck full of Harleys, I can have a horse trailer. I'm sure the country acts do," she laughs.

With her newfound success, Jewel finds that her relationship with her parents is even stronger than ever. She is thrilled to be able to share her musical world with her father, Atz. And she refers to Nedra as her "best friend." Says Jewel of her mother, "Our energies are less focused on surviving, so we can put our energies more into creating. Too much of our lives is wasted on survival."

chapter five

nomore**foolish**games

In her recent past, too much of Jewel's energy was spent dwelling on the hopelessness of her lot in life. Now she finds it all replaced with the shimmering prospect of hope and of attainment. Pondering it all she says, "I never thought that so many people would lend themselves to my dream. Because I lived with such hopelessness for such a long time, I thought it would kill me. You can't live with hopelessness. During a certain phase, it got to the point, when I was 18, just before I lived in my car, why was I going to continue - continue living. I wouldn't say I was suicidal, but I became consciously aware that I could not face time anymore. I think a lot of kids get to that place. You think, 'What the f*** is the point? To have a family? Maybe, maybe not. To be a secretary? Maybe not. To be famous? Probably not.' Even when I was (living) in my car, I hoped I would get to do what I loved. I never thought it would be on this level. I don't mean so much the level of success but the actualization of knowing that for the rest of my life, I'm going to be OK. I'm going to be OK. That's so amazing to get used to."

So many rock stars in the past have gone completely berserk when they finally hit the jackpot. Jewel is quite the opposite. Instead of running through her money barefoot, she is taking a very sane and conservative course with its management and with her spending. With reference to remaining grounded, she claims, "I don't adore 'the biz' and I'm terrified of decadence, so I surround myself with what I know is real. I travel with things that remind me of home, like rocks and eagle feathers, and always remember to be joyful and thankful." Instead of getting a big head about her fame, Jewel is almost embarrassed when fans gush too much about her beauty and her talent. "People look at me in magazines and feel like I'm a phenomenon, as if what I've accomplished is beyond their ability. I tell them to knock it off. If you respect what I've done, then do something yourself," she says.

Jewel further explains, "What someone gets out of the way I lived my life can be immediately diminished by them thinking that I'm a phenomenon. I'm not a phenomenon. I didn't think I was this talented. It wasn't until I really decided, talent or no talent, I have to do what makes me feel like a real person. I would be absolutely useless on stage if people look at me like a phenomenon. It makes me so scared that I could cry right now."

On the
other hand, the
success that she has
experienced has given her a
great deal of self-confidence. She is
obviously a very creative soul, so what is it
that made her choose to pursue music as opposed to
acting or painting? "It's probably just in my blood," she
says. "I feel most myself when I'm on stage, when I'm singing or
when I'm writing. I was raised doing it; I'm just one link on the chain.
Secondly, I got into this versus other arts because it's one of the last real, living
art forms that still has big influence. A lot of the other arts are too easily
intellectualized."

Although fame and fortune are two greatly desirable manifestations in an artist's life, they can also
magnify the pressure to produce. How is Jewel handling the weight that fame has thrust upon her shoulders?
Well, first of all, there is a sense of disbelief. When she is out in public, and a fan starts lauding praise on her, she is

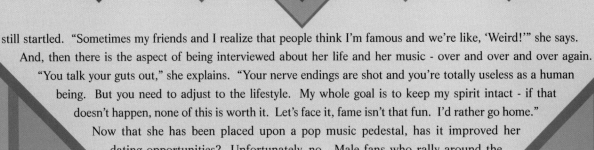

still startled. "Sometimes my friends and I realize that people think I'm famous and we're like, 'Weird!'" she says.
And, then there is the aspect of being interviewed about her life and her music - over and over and over again.
"You talk your guts out," she explains. "Your nerve endings are shot and you're totally useless as a human
being. But you need to adjust to the lifestyle. My whole goal is to keep my spirit intact - if that
doesn't happen, none of this is worth it. Let's face it, fame isn't that fun. I'd rather go home."
Now that she has been placed upon a pop music pedestal, has it improved her
dating opportunities? Unfortunately, no. Male fans who rally around the
front of the stage during one of her shows, rarely show up at the
stage door with candy and flowers. "I'll be doing a show in
Paris and see all these beautiful guys and know that I'll
never get to talk to them because they'll never
find me. They'll never talk to me, they'll
never come up to me. It's okay,
though it is kind of
ironic," she says
with a smile.

She is so
u n d e n i a b l y
beautiful, and has been
praised so heavily for her
looks, has this added undue pressure
to her career?   Do her looks tend to
overshadow the substance and emotion of her
music?   "I think just as a woman in the world - even pre-
fame, at a very early age - most of us are touched by that, the
manipulations of which, I would say, come mainly from the media. Ideas
of beauty," she ponders.   "A lot of women (feel their) worth is in their ability to
seduce.   I wouldn't say that I was exempt from feeling those pressures, especially as a
younger woman.   And now the pressure, once I'm in the business, to be confidently, perfectly
fit and have the personal trainers - everybody starts doing crazy things to their bodies.   I think that's
kinda devastating, because it's creating impossible standards of beauty."

Do her looks eclipse her credibility?   "I think people are too worried about credibility," says Jewel.   "People can
become so worried about being credible, about being rock musicians who don't look like rock musicians.   I really love
what I do, and that's not very popular; I feel fortunate to be in this position.   I'm brave in my living, I'll make mistakes.   Like
the dress for the Grammys."

Is it difficult to be an independent and very focused woman in show business?   According to her, "The limitations women face are probably ever-
present, but I don't think I've ever felt that they were more substantial than what blacks or gays or certain men face."

She is also gratified to have found an audience all of her own, and to find that her fans are very loving and supportive.   The majority of
them feel that Jewel has illuminated a part of their spirits as well.   As she explains it, "My fans are very polite.   People come to my
shows with signs that say, 'Maintaining Our Innocence.'   Cheesy as shit, but 'Hallelujah!'   Look, I'm not fluffy, New Age...
kookybaka (sic).   I'm just a person who is honestly living my life and asking, 'How do you be spiritual and live in the
world without going to a monastery?'   I just want to tell kids, 'Come on, man, get excited!'   There have always
been wars and pollution and poverty, but we're at the most unique time in the history of humanity to do
something about it.   We're worrying less about survival, and more and more about what is our
spirit.   Every kid is asking me about that right now."

A list of Jewel's favorite things helps one to understand the inner workings of her artistic
soul.   When asked to name her favorite poet, she replies, "Pablo Neruda.   He did
a lot of political writing, but his love poems are my favorite - they're like
nothing else in the universe."

And, the question of her favorite mode of transportation is
predictably answered, "Horse.   I used to ride mine to
work and to school sometimes.   I think
everybody should ride something that's
living instead of something
t h a t ' s   e m i t t i n g
e x h a u s t ."

When she is not in a recording studio or a concert hall, Jewel rarely listens to music. She appreciates the silence. However, she claims, "If I had to listen to one kind of music all the time, I would go for Baroque classical music. It's so beautiful. I like Vivaldi's 'Four Seasons' and the requiems of Mozart. But I also listen to punk a lot." Her own music, and her own writing are however two things she approaches with true sincerity. "Music is not a casual thing for people," she claims. "It helps them through very serious things."

Thankfully, her legion of fans will be happy to know that her newfound success hasn't stifled her ability to compose new songs. According to Jewel, "I feel most myself when I sing. I constantly skip around my hotel room going, 'I'm a writer. That's what I do. I write.'"

Freed from the pressures of wondering where her next meal is coming from, or if she has enough money for gasoline, Jewel feels that she is soaring, both spiritually and creatively. "This is my life now," she happily explains. "The amount I'm getting out of it personally and what I'm learning has made me grow by leaps and bounds. I'm greedy with that."

There was once a time in her life when she was clouded in frustration and confusion. She felt the need to create, and to write down all of her thoughts and her perceptions. Now that her life is in high gear, she finds that she still has the same creative energy, and the same drive to write, but without the angst. "I feel at peace. I'm not tortured anymore," Jewel explains. She is now free to write and perform with a revitalized sense of self-worth. She is free to take on the new challenges that film acting, and autobiographical writing are presenting to her.

Just as her American Indian "uncle" had predicted, Jewel is on a lifelong mission to bring truth, honesty, and purity to the souls of all who are touched by her insightful music. She is a voice to illuminate the dark reaches of the human heart, and to unleash enlightenment. Part feminist, part social activist, part innocent poet in a harsh world, her music is a shimmering affirmation to all who hear her songs of vitality and integrity. She is a radiant star in a galaxy of mere singers. At long last she has found her ideal setting to show off her vast singing and writing talents. She is Jewel.